Subject: Jokes
by Jenny Alexander

10:02

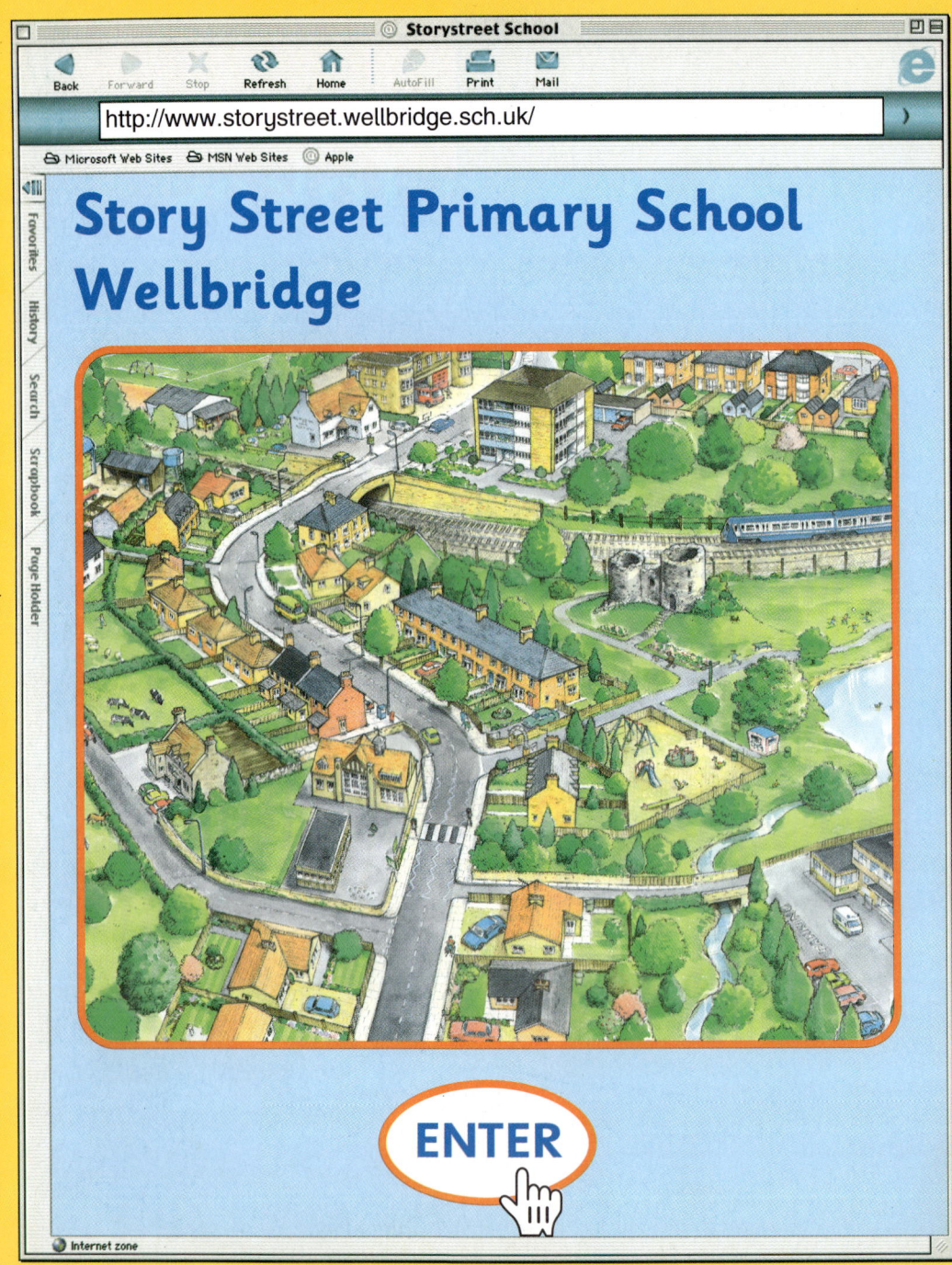

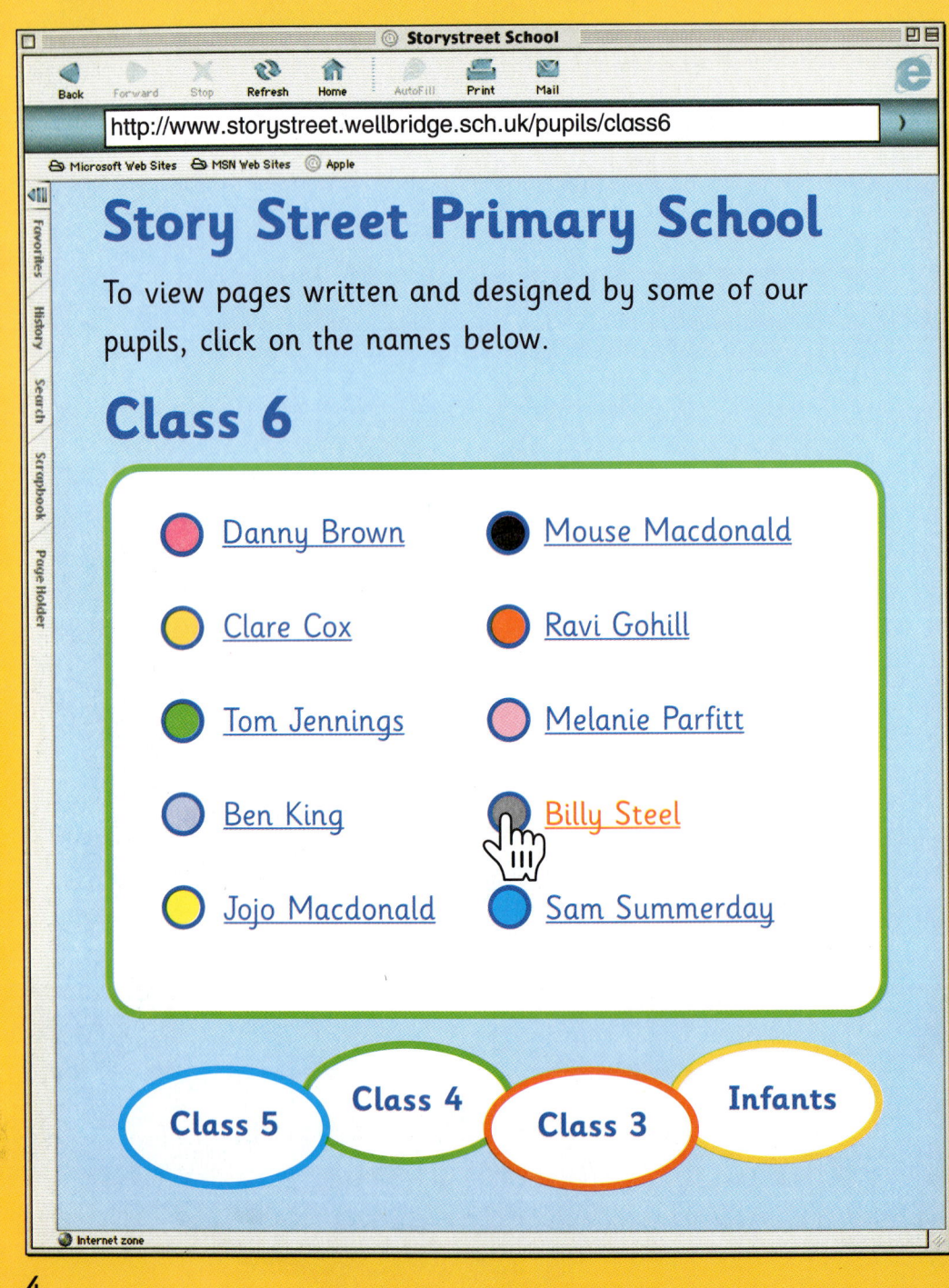

BILLY'S WEB PAGE

Name: Billy Steel **Age: 10**

I've got a big brother called Mick and a little sister called Jasmine. We used to have a hamster called Hercules, but he died. My favourite colour is blue.

My favourite food is pizza. My favourite animal is a monkey.

My best friend is called Ravi. We do a jokes page in our school newsletter.

It's raining cats and dogs: *I know. I trod in a poodle!*

Please drive slowly through the village. One person gets run over every week — and he's getting mighty sick of it!

If you know any good jokes, please send them to me. My school email address is

billysteel/class6@storystreet.wellbridge.sch.uk

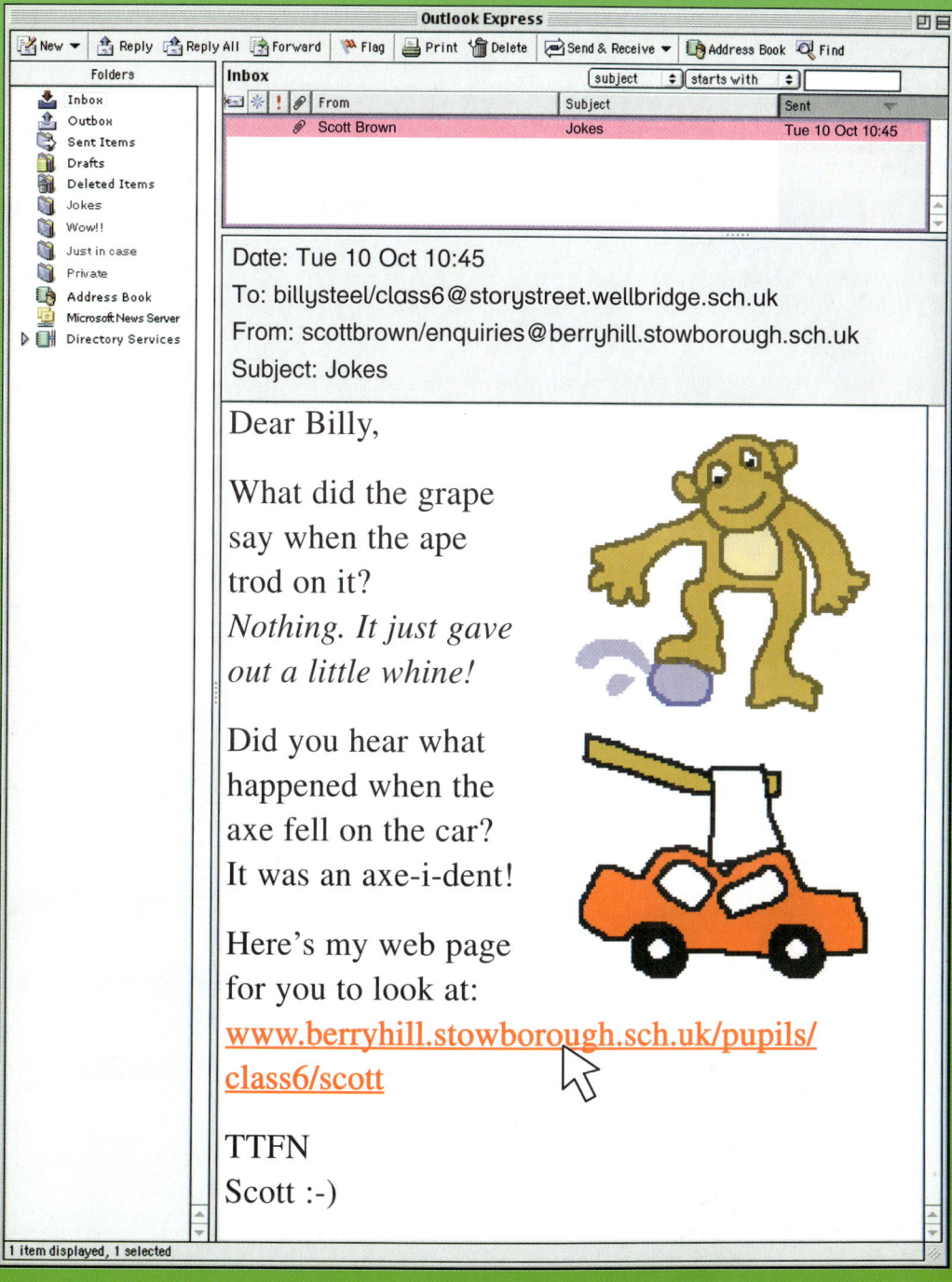

Scott Brown's Web Page

I'm in Year 6, and my teacher is Mrs Parry. She is the best teacher in the entire universe. She also checks our web pages. I've got 24 brothers and 30 sisters and we live in a shoe. Our mum is weak on cooking but strong on discipline.

My favourite animal is an ant,
but don't tell him or he'll get big-headed.

You can write to me if you like –

scottbrown/enquiries@berryhill.stowborough.sch.uk

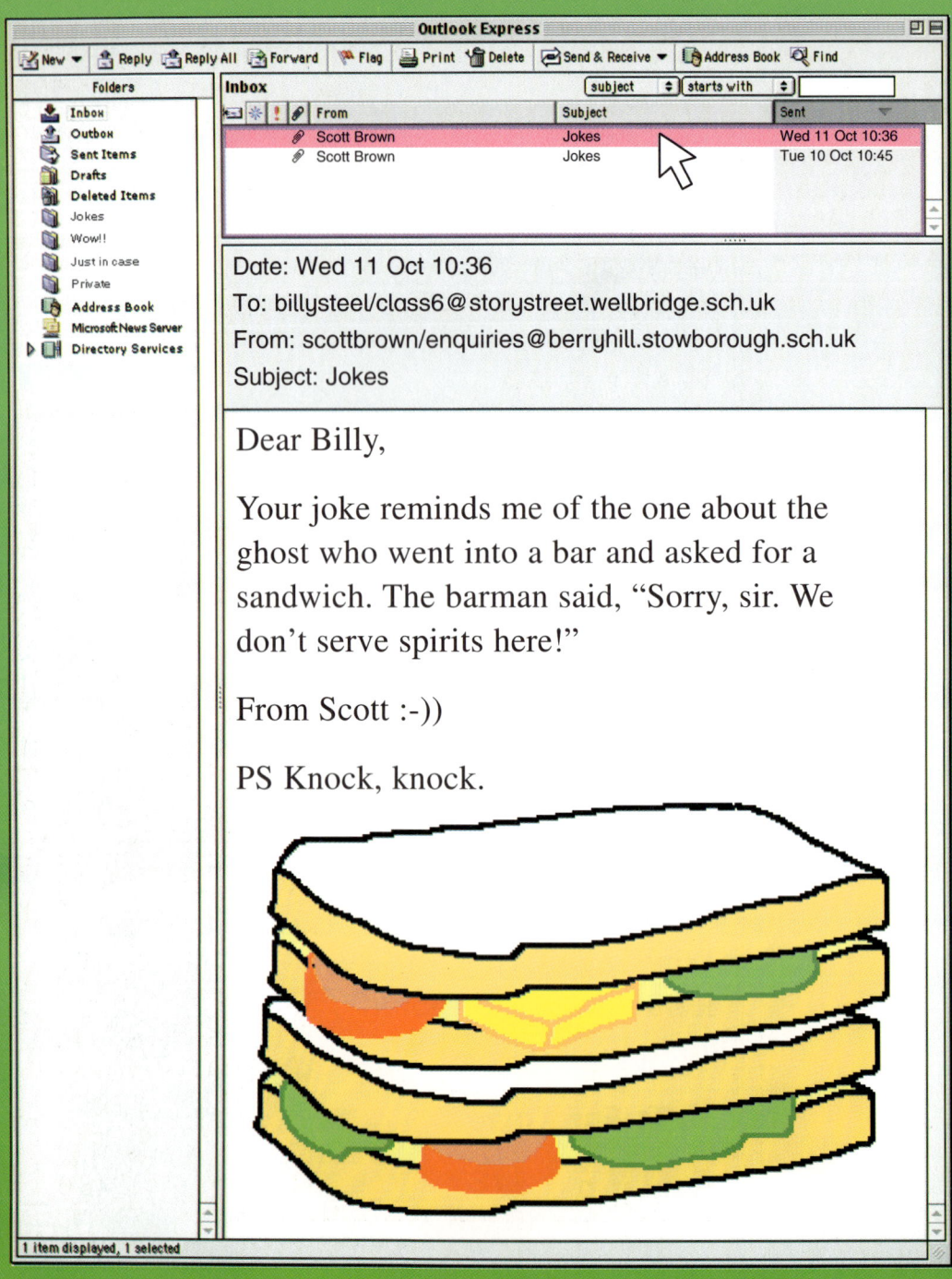

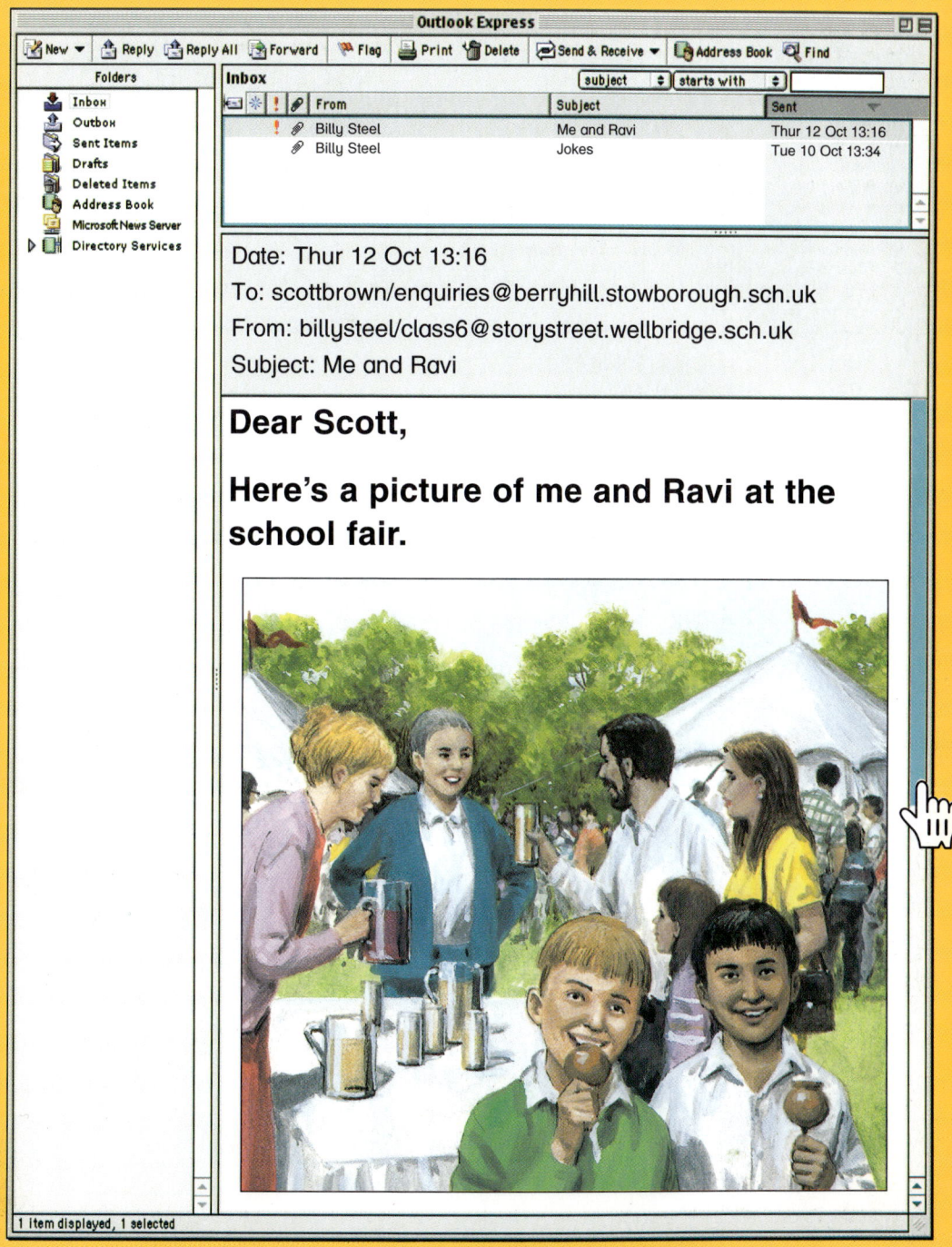

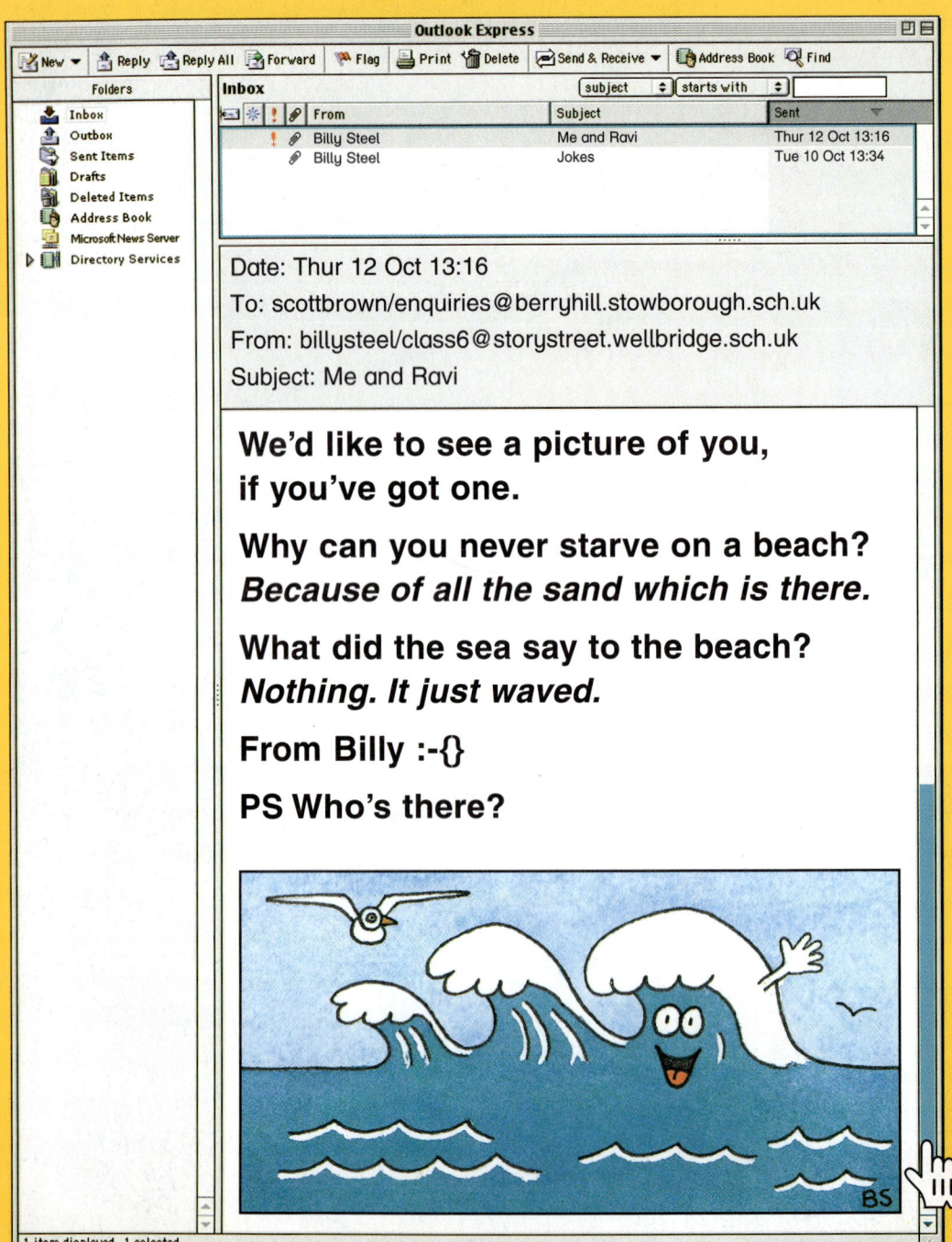

A man at Animal World gave me these for being brave.

Flat 5
York House
Seeward Street
Stowborough
SB5 3HL

Saturday
14th October

Dear Billy,

I fell off a camel yesterday and broke my leg, so I'm going to be off school for a while. That means I won't be able to email you.

If you like, we can still send jokes to each other by snail mail, though.

13

The casualty department was really crowded and we had to wait for ages. I asked everyone to tell me their favourite doctor, doctor joke. This is mine:

Doctor, doctor - I've had this cough for seven days.

Don't worry, laddie. It's just a wee cold!

From

Scott

PS Boo!

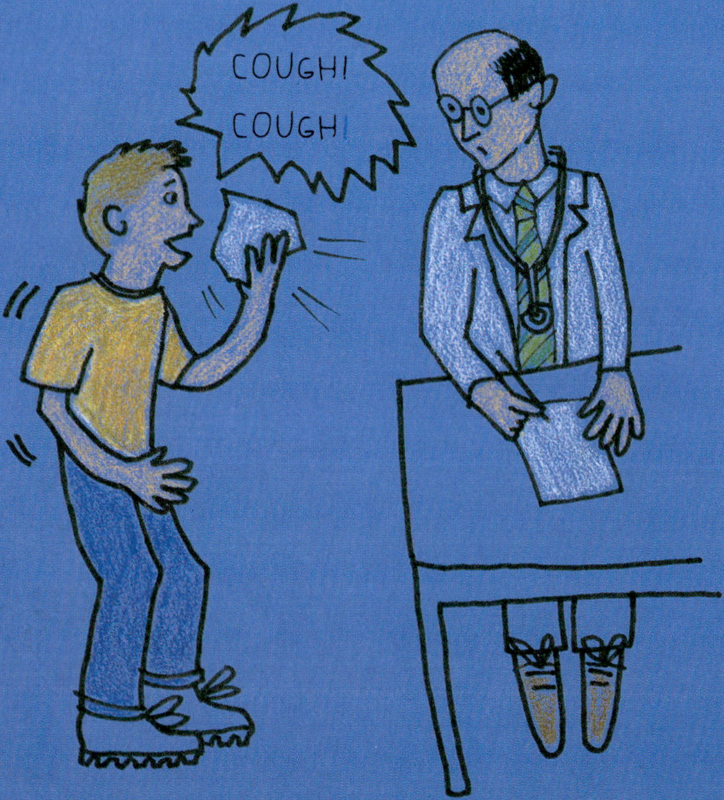

27 Story Street
Wellbridge
WB4 HS2

Friday
20th October

Dear Scott,

Ha, ha! Pull the other one! Why are you really off school? Ravi reckons you've just got flu or something.

Did you hear about the budgie that got flu?

It needed some tweetment!

Found this in Castle Park, but I don't think it's from a budgie.

We can use the post, until you get back to school.

From Billy

PS Boo who?

PPS This is going to be the slowest knock, knock joke ever!

Get Well

Soon

Flat 5
York House
Seeward Street
Stowborough
SB5 3HL

Wednesday 25th October

Dear Billy,

There's no need to cry — it's only a joke!

But the camel thing isn't. I really <u>did</u> fall off it. We were at Animal World, and in the Africa part they do camel rides.

So I'm on this camel, and it's pitching around like a ship in a storm. Have you ever noticed how much camels sway when they walk? Then my stupid sister offers it a lick of her ice cream. (I've only got one sister really, Dawn.)

Drool!

The camel leans forward, then I fall off, and there's this big panic. Mum and Dad come running up the path like a couple of Olympic sprinters, with a gang of people in uniforms at their heels. If the camel steps on me with its great flat feet, I'm a gonner!

Dawn, on the other hand, finds it hilarious. She takes a photo. Here it is.

From

Scott

Now do you believe me? (PS I would like the ticket back please for my scrapbook.)

Get better soon.

27 Story Street
Wellbridge
WB4 HS2

Monday
30th October

Dear Scott,

OK, we believe you.

What do you call a camel at the North Pole?

Lost!

Ravi's a bit worried about your education now that you've only got lessons two mornings a week. So he's sending you a maths question.

Hello! I'm Ravi.

If I had five oranges in one hand and three in the other, what would I have?

Enormous hands!

What do you call a camel with three humps?

Humphrey!

From

Billy

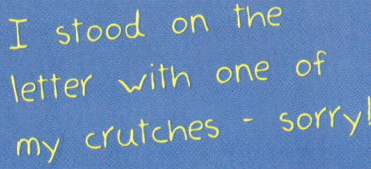

I stood on the letter with one of my crutches – sorry!

Flat 5
York House
Seeward Street
Stowborough
SB5 3HL

Friday 3rd November

Dear Billy,

Keep sending the jokes — I need them! But no more camel jokes please. I'm getting enough of those from Dawn. She says it gives her the hump me sitting around, watching TV all day, when she's got to go to school.

Hi – I am Dawn!

I'm getting the hang of using crutches now, so with a bit of luck I can go back to school soon. It's so boring being stuck at home.

From

Scott

I found this in the local paper:

Stowborough Over 60s Club

Results of the competition for the Most Unusual Object Found on a Beach:
1. Mrs Drayton
2. Mr O'Hara
3. Miss Marks

27 Story Street
Wellbridge
WB4 HS2

Friday
10th November

Dear Scott,

Thanks for your letter. It took us ages to see why the newspaper cutting was funny. It's because it sounds as if the most unusual object found on the beach was Mrs Drayton, right?

One of our friends, Sam, is mad about animals and she wants to know if the camel is all right.

If we were there, Ravi and I would write jokes on your plaster. Can you choose a couple of these, and do it for us?

From

Billy

What's tall and smells nice? A giraffe-odil!

Boy on the beach — A crab's just bitten my toe off.
Mother — Which one?
Boy — I don't know. Crabs all look the same to me!

What is Australian beer made from? Kangaroo hops!

Sister – Oh, no! I made a lovely cake and the cat's eaten it!
Brother – Never mind. I'm sure Mum can get us another cat!

What's big, yellow and wobbly? The trifle tower!

Where do dogs have to keep quiet? In a no-barking zone!

Beekeeper – someone who likes to keep buzzy.

What do you call a gorilla with a bunch of lettuce in each ear? Whatever you like – he can't hear you!

Flat 5
York House
Seeward Street
Stowborough
SB5 3HL

Monday 20th November

Dear Billy,

Tell your friend, Sam, the camel's fine, but I don't think they're letting it give rides any more. I couldn't decide which jokes I liked best, so I wrote them all on my plaster. When I went back to school today, everyone in the class wanted to add a joke, too.

The class made me a 'Welcome Back' banner — this is the first letter from it.

This is what my plaster looks like now.
When they take it off, I'm going to ask if I can keep it.

From

Scott

```
>>>> Date: 28 Nov 10:47
>>>> To: Billy Steel/class6@storystreet.wellbridge.sch.uk
>>>> From: Scott Brown/enquiries@berryhill.stowborough.sch.uk
>>>> Subject: Jokes
>>>>
>>>>
```

>>>> **Dear Billy,**
>>>> **Knock, knock.**
>>>> **From Scott :-))**

```
>>> Date: 28 Nov 10:50
>>> To: Scott Brown/enquiries@berryhill.stowborough.sch.uk
>>> From: Billy Steel/class6@storystreet.wellbridge.sch.uk
>>> Subject: Jokes
>>>
>>>
```

>>> **Hi Scott!**
>>> **Who's there?**
>>> **From Billy :-}**

```
>> Date: 28 Nov 10:52
>> To: Billy Steel/class6@storystreet.wellbridge.sch.uk
>> From: Scott Brown/enquiries@berryhill.stowborough.sch.uk
>> Subject: Jokes
>>
>>
```

>> **Emma**

Printed at 10:59 - 28 Nov   Page 1 of 2

```
> Date: 28 Nov 10:53
> To: Scott Brown/enquiries@berryhill.stowborough.sch.uk
> From: Billy Steel/class6@storystreet.wellbridge.sch.uk
> Subject: Jokes
>
>
```
> **Emma who?**

Date: 28 Nov 10:54
To: Billy Steel/class6@storystreet.wellbridge.sch.uk
From: Scott Brown/enquiries@berryhill.stowborough.sch.uk
Subject: Jokes

Emma Back Online!

Printed at 10:59 - 28 Nov   Page 2 of 2